Drug Abuse and Society™

COCAINE
Coke and the War on Drugs

ROSEN
PUBLISHING®
New York

Linda Bickerstaff

Published in 2009 by The Rosen Publishing Group, Inc.
29 East 21st Street, New York, NY 10010

Library of Congress Cataloging-in-Publication Data

Bickerstaff, Linda.
Cocaine: coke and the war on drugs / Linda Bickerstaff.—1st ed.
    p. cm.—(Drug abuse and society)
Includes bibliographical references and index.
ISBN-13: 978-1-4358-5014-9 (library binding)
1. Cocaine—History. 2. Cocaine abuse. 3. Cocaine abuse—Treatment.
4. Coca—History. I. Title.
HV5810.B53 2009
362.29'8—dc22

                                                      2008012604

Manufactured in Malaysia

Contents

INTRODUCTION

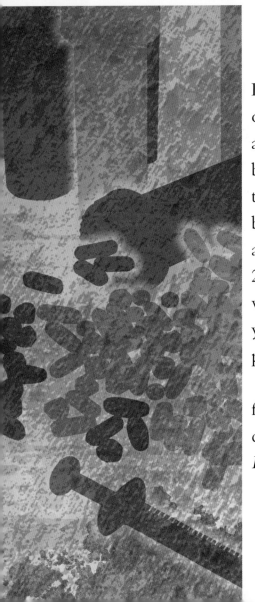

Drug abuse—what is it? A drug is any chemical that is used as a medicine or in making medicine. Drug abuse is the overuse or improper use of drugs for nonmedical purposes. Drug abuse is thought by many to be the single biggest problem in society worldwide today. *The World Drug Report 2007*, issued by the United Nations Office on Drugs and Crime, points out that globally, about 200 million people, or 5 percent of the world's population, use illegal drugs each year. Of this number, 0.6 percent of the people are "problem drug users."

Supplying illegal drugs means big bucks for those who sell the drugs and enormous costs for everyone else. *The World Drug Report 2007* disclosed that in 2005 the actual dollar amount of illicit drug sales worldwide was about 320 billion U.S. dollars. To put that estimate in perspective, compare it to the earnings of four American companies that do business throughout the world, as reported by the investment advisory service Hoovers. McDonald's Corporation earned $21.6 billion, and Coca-Cola earned $24.1 billion in 2006. The Gap, Inc., had sales totaling $15.9 billion in 2006, while Nike, Inc., sold $21.6 billion in shoes and other products that year. These companies' earnings, even if combined, are minimal in comparison to the amount of money made by drug cartels that supply illegal drugs.

The costs of drug abuse are huge. The U.S. National Drug Intelligence Center reported in the *National Drug Threat Assessment 2006* that in 2002, the economic cost of drug abuse to the United States was $180.9 billion.

Whether you call it "bopper," "California cornflakes,"

Cocaine, commonly called "snow" or "blow" in its powder form, is the most abused major stimulant drug in the United States and most European countries today.

"devil's dandruff," "happy dust," "nose candy," or one of the other 165 street names for this illegal drug, you are talking about cocaine. It is derived from the coca plant and is credited with starting and perpetuating drug abuse in the United States. The Substance Abuse and Mental Health Services Administration's (SAMHSA) *National Survey on Drug Use and Health* noted that 20.4 million Americans (8.3 percent of the population) used illicit drugs in 2006. Of those, 2.4 million used cocaine.

Cocaine remains the drug of choice for many drug abusers. It is frequently mixed with alcohol or other drugs for maximum effect, and it is highly addictive. Cocaine is the focus of many federal and state laws, several of which are presently being reviewed and revised. Cocaine is also being studied extensively by scientists seeking ways to curb cocaine addiction. Almost 150 years after it was first extracted from coca, cocaine remains a scourge on society.

CHAPTER 1

Coca to Cocaine: A Historical Overview

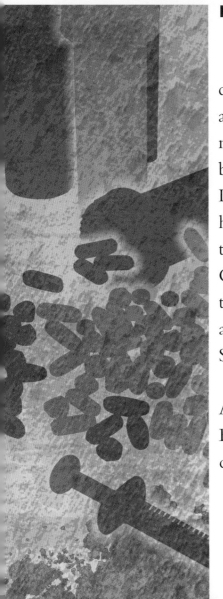

The history of the extraction of cocaine from coca leaves and cocaine's eventual rise to its present status as drug of choice evolved over a period of about 150 years. The coca plant, which is native to the Andes of South America, belongs in the plant family *Erythroxylaceae*. Leaves of the coca plant are chewed as an herbal medicine by the people who live in the mountainous regions of Peru, Colombia, Bolivia, and Ecuador. Chewing the leaves of the coca plant for medicinal and ritual purposes has been a tradition in South America for centuries.

Hunter-gatherers, who first came to the Andean regions in approximately 20,000 BCE, were probably the first people to use coca. Tombs dating back to 3000 BCE have

This farmer once harvested fruit, coffee, and corn on village property in Bolivia. She now earns $190 (U.S. dollars) per month harvesting coca— three times the average wage in the poorest country in South America.

been found to contain coca leaves, and the Incas were known to use coca in their religious ceremonies. In 1630, Dutch settlers in Brazil sent coca plants to the University of Leiden in the Netherlands for its botanical gardens. This was the first time that any significant amount of coca appeared in Europe. Shortly after, it was also transported to North America.

THE FIRST COCAINE CRAZE

Albert Niemann, who was a German chemist, extracted cocaine from coca leaves in 1859. By 1863, just four years later, the chemical formula for cocaine had been found. That same year, a Corsican named Angelo Mariani produced a concoction that was made from soaking coca leaves in Bordeaux wine. This elixir, dubbed Vin Mariani (Mariani's wine), soon became very popular. Six years later, John Pemberton, who was a physician and pharmacist from Atlanta, Georgia, developed a similar, but even more powerful, drink. He mixed coca leaves and extracts from the highly caffeinated African kola nut with alcohol. In 1886, the alcohol was removed from this drink, and it was marketed under the brand name of Coca-Cola. The original formula contained about 8.5 milligrams of cocaine per drink. That is about one-third of the 20 to 30 milligrams of cocaine found in a single line (the usual quantity of cocaine that is sniffed at one time) of street-grade cocaine today. In 1903, cocaine was removed from coca leaves before these leaves were used to flavor Coca-Cola. The formula for the beverage is reportedly unchanged today.

By 1885, scientists had discovered many of cocaine's medicinal properties. It was found to have numbing properties and the ability to constrict, or make narrower, small blood vessels. These characteristics made cocaine quite useful in surgical procedures,

Coca-Cola, developed in 1886 by John Pemberton with cocaine as one of its main ingredients, was soon the most popular soft drink in the world. Cocaine was removed from Coca-Cola in 1903 when the addictive properties of the drug were recognized.

particularly surgical procedures on the nose, the mouth, and the eyes. It is still used in some operations today. Notable scientists such as Sigmund Freud became addicted to cocaine while trying to determine medical uses for the drug. Under the influence of cocaine, Freud wrote at least four papers in which he spoke in favor of its use in the field of psychiatry.

By 1890, cocaine was being added to many patent medicines. Although people were not cured by these elixirs, users certainly felt better after taking them. Many people became addicted to cocaine because of their use of patent medicines, Vin Mariana, and Coca-Cola.

FEDERAL REGULATION OF COCAINE

The first federal law addressing cocaine and other drugs was the Pure Food and Drug Act of 1906. This law required that manufacturers clearly list cocaine and other habit-forming drugs on product labels, but the law did not make the use of such drugs illegal. The Harrison Narcotics Tax Act, which was passed in 1914, required people who produced, imported, or sold products containing opium or cocaine to pay taxes on the products. It also made it illegal to obtain products containing opium or cocaine without a prescription. After these laws passed, addicts began to seek their drugs wherever they could find them—thus starting the modern-day trade in cocaine, which is now a multibillion-dollar illicit industry.

THE SECOND COCAINE CRAZE

From 1920 until the early 1970s, cocaine abuse was overshadowed by the abuse of other substances—marijuana, heroin, hallucinogens, and methamphetamines. High prices and a short supply of cocaine contributed to this phenomenon. By the early 1970s, people were much more prosperous, so the high cost of cocaine became less of

Crack, made by processing powder cocaine to remove impurities, looks like small rocks or pebbles. When smoked in a pipe, it makes cracking sounds—which is how it got its name.

an issue. They were also ready to try a drug that, by reputation, gave a quick jolt of pure pleasure and increased sexual prowess. Cocaine was soon the prestige drug—abused by wealthy young people, up-and-coming professionals, show-business celebrities, and athletes, not to mention many well-known politicians. A method to increase the purity of cocaine was developed in California in 1976, and crack cocaine became available shortly thereafter. (Crack, a purified form of cocaine, looks like chips of rock and can be smoked.) With these two events, the second cocaine craze hit North America with a vengeance.

By the mid-1980s, the peak of cocaine use, 20 percent of young people between the ages of fifteen and twenty-five admitted to using cocaine. Since that time, cocaine use in all age groups has declined. In the 2005 Monitoring the Future Study reported in the National Institute of Drug Abuse publication *InfoFacts: Crack and Cocaine*, 8 percent of the high school seniors surveyed said they had used cocaine at least once in their lifetimes.

Cocaine's popularity as a drug of abuse has waxed and waned for hundreds of years. Today, it is considered to be the champagne of illicit drugs and remains the most abused major stimulant in the United States.

Myths and Facts

Myth: Cocaine is not an addictive drug.

Fact: Cocaine stimulates pleasure and craving centers in the brain, which is one reason why it is so addictive. Even snorting one line of cocaine can create an undeniable urge to continue its use. It is classified by the U.S. Food and Drug Administration (FDA) as a Schedule II drug because it has very high potential for abuse.

Myth: Cocaine is not very toxic, so few people die of cocaine overdoses.

Fact: Dr. Carmelito Arkangel, in an article on WebMD, reported that the toxic dose of cocaine is unknown. The average lethal dose of injected or snorted cocaine is about 700 to 850 milligrams. The lethal dose is subject to individual variation. He wrote, "Deaths have occurred in doctors' offices with as little as 25 milligrams applied to mucous membranes or the snorting of a single line in recreational use where the average dose of one line is 20 milligrams."

Myth: It is not illegal to drive while using cocaine.

Fact: The National Institute on Drug Abuse (NIDA) *InfoFacts* report says that in twelve states (Arizona, Georgia, Illinois, Indiana, Iowa, Michigan, Minnesota, Nevada, Pennsylvania, Rhode Island, Utah, and Wisconsin) it is illegal for a person to operate a motor vehicle with any detectable level of a prohibited drug or its metabolite in his or her blood. Other state laws define drugged driving as driving when a drug "renders the driver incapable of driving safely" or "causes the driver to be impaired."

CHAPTER 2

From Leaf to Street

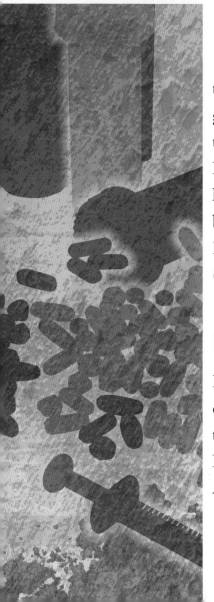

Many new cocaine users discover that it is very easy to get hooked on cocaine but almost impossible to get off of it. They might not have gotten hooked on cocaine if a supply of the drug had not been readily available. Drug traffickers extract cocaine in illegal labs in South America and then smuggle it by various routes into the United States. From there, the people who sell the drugs (pushers) supply their users.

DRUG CARTELS

Ninety-seven percent of the world's cocaine is produced by drug cartels in three countries: Colombia, Peru, and Bolivia. In the *National Drug Threat Assessment 2006*, the U.S. National Drug

Cocaine, and the chemicals used to make it from coca paste, are removed from an illicit cocaine refinery in Rio de Janeiro, Brazil, by a member of a special Brazilian police unit.

Intelligence Center reported that in 2004, 860 tons (780 metric tons) of export-quality (at least 84 percent pure) cocaine were produced in these three countries—two-thirds of it coming from Colombia.

Once produced, cocaine is smuggled into the United States and other countries by several different routes. The *National Drug Threat Assessment 2006* points out that Mexican drug trafficking

In the largest seizure of cocaine in Mexican history, 23.5 tons (21.3 metric tons) of cocaine, found in containers shipped from Colombia, were confiscated and incinerated. A Mexican marine guards the incineration site.

organizations control most of the wholesale cocaine distribution in the United States. In 2006, 744 tons (675 metric tons) of cocaine left South America for the United States. Two hundred and sixteen tons (196 metric tons) were seized in transit—mostly at Mexican borders or at sea. An additional 39 tons (35 metric tons) were seized on arrival in the United States. That means that as many as 491 tons (445 metric tons) of cocaine were available for distribution.

Cocaine passes through the hands of many pushers before it gets to users. At each stage of its transfer, it is likely to be "cut" or "stepped on" (diluted) with additives such as sugar (mannitol, lactose, or glucose), sugar substitutes, talcum powder, cornstarch, or even other drugs. This process increases profits for each pusher.

Purity of the end product can range from 84 percent to 1 percent, depending on how much diluting material is added.

METHODS OF USE

The most common method of use, for first-time and many full-time users, is snorting, or sniffing. A line, or small quantity, of cocaine is quickly inhaled into the nose. With this method, a user will start to feel the effects of the drug quickly. The buzz, or high, will last from one to three hours.

Cocaine can also be dissolved in water and injected directly into veins. This is called slamming or mainlining. Cocaine used in this way gives an almost instantaneous high because the drug is released directly into the bloodstream.

In 1976, a process called freebasing was developed in California. The purpose was to free cocaine of the impurities that had been added in the process of cutting—thus the name freebase. Freebase is usually about 95 percent cocaine. Freebase has a low melting point, so, unlike powdered cocaine that is denatured by heat, it can be smoked. The major disadvantage of freebasing, from the user's standpoint, is that the solvent used in the process (usually ether or ammonia) is highly flammable, which leads to a high risk for fire, as well as unknown risks from inhaling the solvent vapors. The buzz obtained from freebasing occurs very rapidly and is likely equivalent to that obtained by slamming.

The development of crack cocaine contributed more to the upsurge of cocaine use in the 1980s than any other single factor. Crack is made by processing powdered cocaine to form a waxy substance that hardens into "rocks" of cocaine. The rocks can be placed in a pipe and smoked. As it heats up, the mixture begins to snap and crack, which is the origin of its name. Crack is the most commonly used form of cocaine today because it is relatively inexpensive and quite pure.

Cocaine is also mixed with other drugs. Some commonly used combinations include "bazooka" (crack and marijuana); "croak" (cocaine mixed with methamphetamine); "dynamite," "speedball," or "goofball" (cocaine mixed with heroin); and many others. These combinations of drugs can be particularly deadly.

REASONS FOR USE

Many reasons are given for starting to use drugs. Most fall into one of the following categories:

- Because everyone is doing it
- Out of boredom
- To escape from stress and other painful problems
- To rebel
- For instant gratification
- To build confidence and improve self-image

- Because role models use drugs
- To feel grown up
- Curiosity

SIGNS AND SYMPTOMS OF USE

Cocaine's main effect is to stimulate a person's central nervous system (CNS). Every time it is used, it causes dilatation of the pupils of the eyes and elevation of blood pressure, heart rate, respiratory (breathing) rate, and body temperature. It also causes small blood vessels to constrict. The combination of these effects can be catastrophic. Elevated heart rate in the face of high blood pressure and constriction of small vessels can result in heart attacks and strokes that are fatal. These effects can even happen the first time the drug is used.

When small vessels constrict, inadequate amounts of blood and, therefore, inadequate amounts of oxygen being transported in blood are carried to some parts of the body. This may result in tissue death. An example is the development of sores or even holes in the nasal septum, the tissue between the two sides of the nose, in those who snort cocaine on a regular basis. A runny nose and frequent nosebleeds are common among cocaine abusers.

Loss of appetite, sleeplessness, agitation, hallucinations, and paranoia are a few of the other symptoms of its use.

Cocaine use stimulates a person's central nervous system, causing among other things, dilation of the pupils of the eyes.

Some cocaine users claim to be more alert, more productive, and more self-confident when using the drug, but these perceived attributes are usually overshadowed by all its associated complications.

Ten Great Questions to Ask a Doctor

1. How do the health effects of freebase differ from those of crack?
2. Is crack more addictive than powder cocaine?
3. Why is a drug that stimulates a pleasure center in the brain more likely to be addictive than a drug that affects other parts of the brain?
4. If cocaine is not injected, why is a cocaine abuser still at increased risk for contracting HIV?
5. Why is the combination of alcohol and cocaine the most common cause of drug-related deaths?
6. Do the adverse effects of cocaine differ depending on its route of use?
7. Are babies born to mothers who use cocaine ("crack babies") permanently damaged?
8. Why do young, healthy athletes sometimes die suddenly after using cocaine?
9. Can a person get hooked on cocaine after snorting just one line?
10. Is a person who smokes tobacco more likely to use cocaine than one who doesn't smoke?

CHAPTER 3
Addiction and Treatment

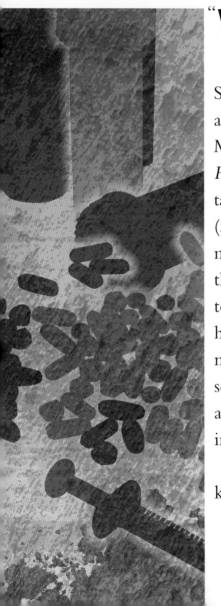

"Way to go!," "We knew you'd win!," and "Congratulations!" echoed through the gym as Sarah arrived for basketball practice shortly after the winners of the National New Models contest had been announced in *Fashion World*. Sarah was 5 feet and 10 inches tall (1.78 meters) and weighed 125 pounds (57 kilograms), about average for a fashion model, but she had never believed she had the right stuff and physical characteristics to be a model. How cool was it that she had just won a year's contract with a top modeling agency, the promise of a college scholarship whenever she chose to use it, and her parents' permission to spend a year in New York City? She was thrilled!

Sarah's first day at the agency was a killer. By the end of the day, she was ready to drop. "Wow!" she said to her new roommate, an experienced model. "Is every day going to be this busy? If so, I understand how you stay so thin." As Sarah was soon to find out, though, hard work had little to do with how thin her roommate was—or how thin Sarah would soon become.

"Snort a line, Sweetie. We need a lot more action in this shot." Sarah had just done a line of coke a few minutes before, but, heeding the orders of the photographer, she took another snort, and another, and another. Sarah had found that she couldn't meet the challenges of her hectic schedule without cocaine.

Sarah's year as a contest winner ended with her appearance as a runway model at the prestigious New York Fashion Festival. Her parents, who hadn't seen her in months, wanted to surprise her, so they waited until the last minute before taking their seats. The lights dimmed, the music rose, and the show started. "That can't be Sarah," her mother whispered to Sarah's dad. "She looks like a cadaver!" But it was Sarah, almost 20 pounds (9 kg) lighter than when her parents had seen her last—a mere 105 pounds (48 kg) of overbearing, irritable fashion model with attitude.

Sarah's parents didn't wait to be invited backstage after the show. They had to see what was wrong with Sarah. They found out as they walked into the dressing room in time to see the exhausted teen snort another needed line of coke. Sarah didn't make the post-show party that night. Her folks wasted no time— she was the newest resident in one of New York's finest drug rehab centers before the party started. Sarah lived to use her college scholarship, but she is haunted to this day with dreams of another line of coke.

HOW COCAINE WORKS ON THE BODY

Cocaine is a central nervous system stimulant that affects pleasure and craving centers in the brain. The brain is made up of millions

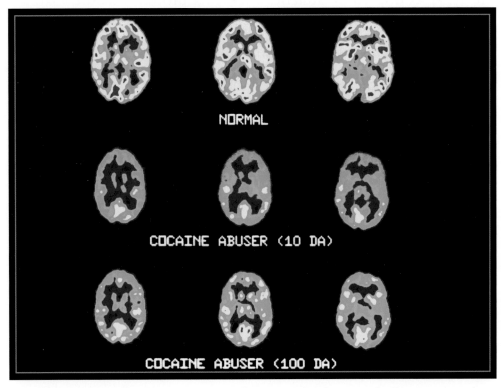

The bright red and yellow areas on the upper brain scan indicate normal metabolic brain activity. Cocaine use causes diminished brain metabolic activity as shown on brain scans taken ten days after cocaine use (middle scan) and one hundred days after use (lower scan).

of nerve cells called neurons. One of the jobs of neurons is to carry impulses from a receptor organ, like the nose, to parts of the brain where interpretation of impulses can be made. Neurons are not actually attached together but are separated by small spaces called synapses. As an impulse passes down one neuron, it doesn't jump across the synapse to the next neuron. It is carried across by a chemical called a neurotransmitter. One of the main neuro-transmitters is dopamine. After it has carried the impulse across the synapse, dopamine attaches itself to a protein called dopamine transporter (DAT). DAT carries dopamine back to the neuron from which it came so it can be reabsorbed and used again.

When a line of coke is snorted, cocaine is absorbed through the nasal mucous membranes into the bloodstream and is carried to the brain, especially to pleasure and craving centers in a part of the brain called the nucleus accumbens. There, it binds to DAT at the sites normally used for binding dopamine. As a consequence, there is a lot of unbound dopamine left in synapses. The dopamine continuously stimulates receiving neurons in the nucleus accumbens, creating the euphoria reported by cocaine users and the cravings that help lead to addiction.

Over time, cocaine abusers develop tolerance to the drug. Higher and more frequent doses of cocaine are needed to produce the same level of pleasure the abuser first experienced. Marilyn, a teen cocaine abuser, in an article entitled "A Deadly Road to Personal Ruin," summed up cocaine abuse with this comment:

Young Cocaine Users and Addiction

Teens are at higher risk for cocaine addiction than are those who first use cocaine as adults because their brains are not as fully developed. A 2001 study conducted by Dr. Judith Rapaport, reported in "Teenage Brain: A Work in Progress" from the National Institute of Mental Health, reported that the cerebral cortex is not fully developed until adulthood. The cerebral cortex, the part of the brain lying just behind the eyes, is responsible for judgment and impulse control. As a result, teens and adolescents may not show good judgment and frequently act impulsively. They do not consider the long-term consequences of what they do. Not thinking of its possible consequences, young people try cocaine "just for fun" and soon find they are hooked.

"With coke, you are like a moth stuck on a light. It attracts you more and more. You can't stop it. It's not physical. It's in your head. The more you have it, the more you want . . ."

FACTORS CONTRIBUTING TO COCAINE ADDICTION

Researchers have been looking for a genetic cause for cocaine addiction for many years. In 2003, Dr. Leslie Jacobsen and colleagues from Yale University found that the gene controlling the production of DAT has two possible forms, or variants. If a person has the variant of the gene called the nine-repeat allele,

DAT production and sensitivity are changed so the person is at high risk for addiction if he or she uses cocaine. A study reported by Dr. Gerome Breen from King's College in London, England, in March 2006 showed that people who have two copies of the nine-repeat allele are 50 percent more likely than those without the variant to become cocaine-dependent if they ever experiment with cocaine. It is hoped that findings like these will eventually lead to more successful treatment options for cocaine addicts.

Children of drug addicts are at risk for both physical and mental abuse. Following the example of their parents, in environments where drugs are readily available, they are also at risk for becoming addicts at early ages.

Environmental factors also contribute to the development of drug addiction. Children who grow up in an environment where drugs are used are at a much higher risk to use drugs themselves. Children may be physically and emotionally abused. They start using drugs to escape from bad situations. They may also get the idea that the use of drugs is normal because their parents or siblings use them.

Societal factors that influence cocaine addiction center around the availability of drugs. If drugs are plentiful and cheap, they are more likely to be used and abused. On the other hand, if society regulates drugs tightly, drugs may be less accessible and, therefore, less likely to be abused. Those who sanction the legalization of drugs disagree with this concept. They believe that it is impossible to keep people who want to use drugs from getting them. It would be better, in their estimation, to legalize drugs, control the purity of the drugs available, tax them, and use the money obtained from taxes for rehabilitation purposes. At the present time, most Americans appear to believe that regulation of addictive drugs is very important.

TREATMENTS FOR COCAINE ADDICTION

There are no medications currently available that are specifically targeted at treating cocaine abuse. Several, however, are in experimental and developmental stages.

Group counseling is often a part of cocaine dependence recovery plans. Plans incorporating peer pressure and bonding are especially effective among teenage addicts.

Dr. Alan Kozikowski, professor of medicinal chemistry at the University of Illinois at Chicago College of Pharmacy, in a November 16, 2007, article on the Web site EurekAlert!, said that most research on drugs to treat cocaine abuse has centered around drugs that affect the action of dopamine. He went on to say, "Success with this particular approach has been marginal at best." The work that Kozikowski is doing involves the neurotransmitter serotonin, which controls a wide variety of behaviors.

New drugs that bind serotonin receptor sites may be potentially therapeutic for treating cocaine addiction.

Another drug, D-cycloserine, which was originally developed as an antibiotic, was reported late in 2007 on News-Medical.net to have potential use in the treatment of cocaine addiction. Very preliminary work on this drug shows that it may help to extinguish the craving experienced by cocaine addicts.

There are several behavioral intervention approaches being used in cocaine rehabilitation programs. Most therapists believe that a defined length of residential (inpatient) treatment followed by long-term outpatient treatment gives the best and most long-lasting results. Perhaps the most important thing that must be done is to tailor the treatment to fit the needs of each individual. If, for example, an addict is unemployed, rehabilitation efforts must include vocational training and career counseling. Homelessness and other social issues must also be addressed. Cocaine addicts are never cured of their addiction. Recovery from cocaine addiction is a lifelong pursuit.

CHAPTER 4

Cocaine and the Law

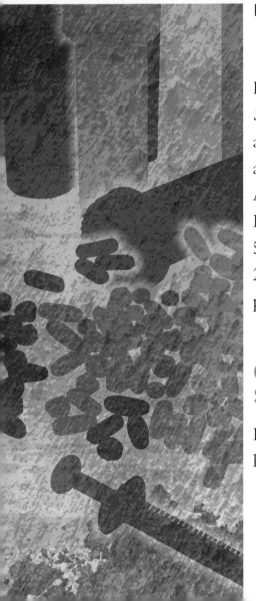

The possession and trafficking of cocaine are felonies in the United States. The Federal Bureau of Investigation's report *Crime in the United States, 2006* states that 117,286 juveniles were arrested by state and local law enforcement agencies for drug abuse violations in 2006. At the federal level, the U.S. Drug Enforcement Administration (DEA) arrested 526 juveniles under the age of nineteen in 2004. Two hundred of those arrests (38 percent) were for cocaine-related offenses.

CONTROLLED SUBSTANCES

In 1970, Congress passed the Comprehensive Drug Abuse Prevention and

In 2004, agents of the U.S. Drug Enforcement Administration (DEA) arrested two hundred juveniles under the age of nineteen on cocaine-related charges.

Control Act, which requires drug manufacturers to safe-guard and maintain records for specific types of drugs. A part of the law, called the Controlled Substances Act, places drugs into one of five categories or schedules based on how the drugs are to be used, safety concerns, and whether they can be addictive. Schedule I substances are those that have no indicated medical use and have a high risk for abuse. Heroin, lysergic acid diethylamide (LSD), mescaline, marijuana, and peyote are all Schedule I substances. Cocaine is a Schedule II drug. It has high potential for abuse but also has some acceptable medical uses such as controlling bleeding. Other Schedule II drugs include opium, methadone, amphetamines, and methamphetamine. Schedule III, IV, and V drugs have progressively less risk for abuse and have accepted medical uses.

DRUG LAWS

Sarah Karp's article "State Drug Law Hits City Teens, Minorities," published in the *Chicago Reporter*, tells of a sixteen-year-old boy named T. J. who was arrested and charged with possession of cocaine with intent to deliver. The arrest was made within 1,000 feet (305 meters) of his former elementary school. Factors that

Cocaine is a Schedule II controlled substance and cannot be legally obtained without a prescription. Pharmacists are required by law to keep strict records of sales of all controlled substances.

will be of major importance to T. J. as he proceeds through the criminal justice system are his age, the severity of the crime for which he was arrested, and the state in which he was arrested.

Age

In the federal court system, juvenile crime is defined as any illegal act committed by a person under the age of eighteen. The age at which a youth can be tried as an adult in state courts varies from state to state. Most teens arrested for cocaine-related offenses are dealt with through the juvenile justice system, where there is a strong emphasis on rehabilitation. Some are sentenced to jail time in juvenile correction facilities, while others are ordered to participate in structured drug rehabilitation programs. Records of their convictions are sealed, so the teens are not negatively affected for the rest of their lives by their felony convictions.

The brain is not fully developed until a person is about twenty-five years old. In an article written by Malcolm Ritter for the Associated Press, Dr. Laurence Steinberg, professor of psychology at Temple University, said that the teenage brain is like a car with a good accelerator but weak brakes. Young people act impulsively, do not show good judgment when excited or stressed, and are unable to appreciate the long-term consequences of their actions. These facts are now being considered by authorities and legislators who are modifying juvenile sentencing laws.

Those who support these changes believe teens should not be subjected to adult punishment regardless of their crimes. Those who do not support juvenile sentencing reform believe that too many juvenile criminals commit outrageous acts because they know they will be tried in the juvenile system rather than in adult courts.

How a defense of "immaturity" will ultimately affect state juvenile sentencing laws is unknown, but it has influenced federal law. In March 2005, the U.S. Supreme Court ruled the death penalty unconstitutional for persons under the age of eighteen.

Severity of the Crime

Had T. J. been arrested for possession of cocaine alone, a Class D felony, he would have been tried in juvenile court. His offense was more serious than that, though. He was arrested with enough cocaine in his possession to make authorities believe he intended to sell it. He was also arrested within 1,000 feet (305 m) of a school. Those two factors make his offense a Class A felony. The state of Illinois, as well as many other states, automatically assigns juveniles who are age fifteen or older to adult court if they are accused of Class A felonies. Michelle Calderon, a staff writer for AnaiRhoads.org, reported that in Vermont and Wisconsin, children as young as ten can be tried in adult courts if their crimes are especially vicious.

Juveniles who are convicted of possessing and/or trafficking in drugs may be jailed in either juvenile or adult prisons. These teens await evaluation prior to imprisonment.

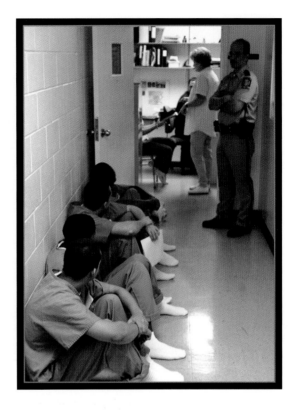

If they are convicted in adult court, juveniles can receive the same sentences as adults or they can receive blended sentences. With blended sentences, young people are jailed in juvenile facilities until age seventeen or eighteen and are then transferred to adult prisons. If authorities feel they have been adequately rehabilitated in juvenile facilities, the adult prison portion of sentences can be cancelled.

Juveniles can even be given adult probation without doing jail time. The conditions of probation are set by a judge and may include community service (labor done in the community for a public agency or a nonprofit organization without pay), attendance at a drug rehabilitation program, or other requirements. Probation may last as long as five years. Regardless, the records of juveniles convicted in adult courts are not sealed. Their felony convictions will haunt them for the rest of their lives.

Felons Lose Rights

Convicted felons lose many rights enjoyed by other citizens of the United States. They can no longer vote or hold public office. They may also be given the following restrictions:

- Be denied admission to professional schools (law school, medical school, etc.)
- Be denied a license by the state for certain professions
- Be denied the opportunity to take civil service exams
- Be excluded from military academies and serving in the military
- Be denied the opportunity to become a citizen of another country
- Be denied a U.S. passport

The State in Which a Person Is Convicted

With the advent of crack cocaine in the early 1980s, drug use and abuse almost reached epidemic proportions in the United States. To get tough on crime, Congress passed the Anti–Drug Abuse Act of 1986. The act contained mandatory minimal sentencing guidelines—the very same guidelines Congress had previously removed from federal law in 1970. The guidelines made specific jail sentences mandatory for drug dealers and also for those in possession of certain amounts of drugs. Although federal mandatory minimal sentencing laws were offered as guidelines, states did not necessarily enact the same standards. This is why the state in which one is convicted is important.

According to the authors of *Illicit Drug Policies: Selected Laws from the 50 States*, as reported by the Robert Woods Johnson Foundation, "The variation [in state laws] is particularly noticeable in the range of penalties for the sale and possession of standard retail amounts of cocaine . . . For instance, in North Carolina, a drug offender charged with selling one gram of cocaine could be subject to a maximum imprisonment term of one year. The same sales offense in Montana could be met with a maximum fine of $50,000 and a lifetime sentence."

The concept of mandatory minimum sentencing laws is now being reviewed in many states. Those who support continuing these laws believe that they are good because, at the very least, they allow for consistency of sentencing within a state. Those who oppose these laws say that they transfer sentencing power from judges, who are supposedly impartial, to prosecutors, who are not. Dennis W. Archer, former mayor of Detroit and a Michigan Supreme Court justice, in an article written for the American Bar Association, said, "The idea that Congress [or state legislators] can dictate a one-size-fits-all sentencing scheme does not make sense. Judges need to have the discretion to weigh the specifics of the cases before them and determine an appropriate sentence. There is a reason we give judges a gavel, not a rubber stamp."

THE CRACK VERSUS POWDER COCAINE CONTROVERSY

One of the best examples of how state policies differ from federal policy, and from one another, is the dissimilarity between sentences for the possession or sale of powder cocaine and crack cocaine. Alexandra Marks, in an article published in the *Christian Science*

In a meeting held December 11, 2007, the U.S. Sentencing Commission voted to make more lenient sentences for crack cocaine offenses retroactive. Above, Judge Ricardo H. Hinojosa, chairman of the commission, announces the results of the commission's vote. Almost twenty thousand federal inmates are eligible for reduced sentences.

Monitor in 2007, wrote, "Since 1988, possession of five grams of crack cocaine—an amount equal to five packets of sugar substitute—landed a person in jail for five years. But people caught with cocaine powder would have to possess 100 times that amount, or 500 grams, to get the same five-year stint behind bars."

The 100:1 ratio, as it is known, came under fire almost as soon as it was enacted. The U.S. Sentencing Commission, a group charged with recommending sentences for various crimes, has, on four occasions, recommended to Congress that this law be changed. Congress has not acted on that recommendation. On November 1, 2007, the Sentencing Commission officially reduced its recommended sentences for crack-related offenses. Marks said, "As a result, up to 4 in 5 people found guilty of crack cocaine offenses will get sentences that are, on average, 16 months shorter than they would have been under the former guidelines." On December 11, 2007, the commission voted to make the more lenient sentences retroactive. This action went into effect on March 3, 2008. About twenty thousand federal prisoners were impacted by these changes.

CHAPTER 5

Cocaine's Cost to Society

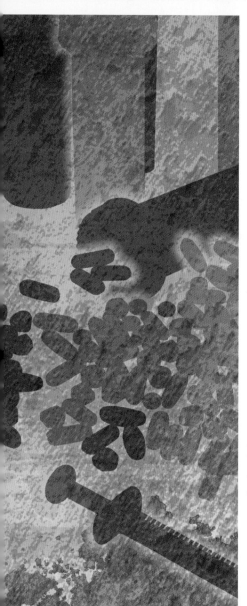

The National Institute on Drug Abuse (NIDA) issued a comprehensive study of the impact of drugs on society in 1992. According to that study, the economic cost of drug abuse (excluding tobacco and alcohol abuse) to American society in 1992 was $97.7 billion. The Office of National Drug Control Policy (ONDCP) issued a publication in 2004 entitled *The Economic Costs of Drug Abuse in the United States 1992–2002*, which used data from the 1992 NIDA report to estimate the economic costs of drug abuse in 2002. According to the ONDCP report, the economic cost of drug abuse increased an average of 5.3 percent per year from 1992 to 2002. The actual dollar estimate for 2002 was $180.9 billion.

A judge presides over a Texas Drug Diversion Court. Drug courts were devised to reduce substance abuse and criminal behavior without imprisoning nonviolent drug offenders.

CRIME-RELATED COSTS OF DRUG ABUSE TO SOCIETY

About half of the total cost reported by NIDA was for crime-related expenses. These included the cost of arresting, prosecuting, and imprisoning drug-crime offenders. They also included the cost of paying for programs such as drug courts. In its special report entitled *Drug Courts: The Second Decade (2006)*, the National Institute of Justice states that the goal of drug courts is to reduce substance abuse and criminal behavior among nonviolent drug offenders without imprisoning them. Drug court programs vary, but they emphasize education, job training, and the development of life skills while also closely monitoring participants for drug use. In 2006, each participant in a drug court cost society an average of $5,928. Imprisoning a drug offender is much more expensive, costing between $20,000 and $50,000 per year.

HEALTH CARE COSTS

NIDA reported that health care expenditures for drug abuse problems cost about $9.9 billion in 1992. Half of that was spent for acute abuse treatment, detoxification, rehabilitation services, prevention measures, education about drugs, and research efforts to find ways to prevent addiction. The ONDCP estimated health care expenditures related to drug abuse to be $16 billion in 2002. Funding for increased numbers of community-based treatment programs and the treatment of an increasing number of drug abusers with HIV/AIDS accounted for much of the increase in health care costs.

Increased numbers of visits to hospital emergency departments also contributed to increased costs. A report from the Substance Abuse and Mental Health Services Administration's (SAMHSA) Drug Abuse Warning Network (DAWN) states that in the last six months of 2003, there were 332,046 emergency department visits related to "drug misuse or abuse." Fifty-four percent of them involved the use of multiple drugs, and 65 percent involved the use of alcohol with at least one other drug. Cocaine was the most frequently abused drug (other than alcohol) for those visiting emergency rooms and accounted for 28 percent of visits.

Although it varies from hospital to hospital, emergency department bills are steep. Anessa Myers, writing for the *Goldsboro (NC) News-Argus,* said that Wellbrook Blue Cross-Blue Shield, a provider of medical insurance, reported that in 2007, the average bill for an emergency department visit was $1,049. In 2007 dollars, the 2003 emergency department visit made for cocaine-related health problems alone would have cost almost $98 million.

Increase in drug abuse has resulted in an increase in the spread of diseases such as hepatitis C and human immunodeficiency virus (HIV). Health care costs for treating these illnesses are massive. Teens often think that if they don't inject cocaine or other drugs, they will not be at added risk for needle-borne infections such as HIV. That is true, but cocaine use is often associated with promiscuous sexual activity, one of the main risk factors for the spread of HIV and other sexually transmitted diseases. Some cocaine addicts (both male and female) trade sex for drugs.

Unplanned pregnancies among female cocaine abusers also add to health care costs. Prenatal problems such as high blood pressure and seizures are not uncommon in females who are addicted to cocaine. In the late 1980s, it was thought that "crack babies," babies born to cocaine-addicted mothers, would have many permanent impairments. These babies often require very expensive hospital care immediately after birth, and some children exposed to cocaine in the womb will ultimately experience developmental problems.

THE COSTS OF COCAINE REHABILITATION PROGRAMS

The Office of National Drug Control Policy reported that about two million teens between the ages of fifteen and seventeen needed treatment for alcohol and drug abuse in 2006. Fewer than 200,000 actually obtained treatment.

In 2002, SAMHSA said that residential (in-patient) treatment for alcohol and drug abuse cost $3,840 per admission, while outpatient treatment costs were about $1,432 per course of treatment. Many experts believe that treatment, especially for juveniles, needs to combine both inpatient and outpatient programs. Even with the high cost of these programs, it is less expensive and much more effective to rehabilitate young people than to imprison them.

Richard Scheinin, writing for the Robert Woods Johnson Foundation's Silent Treatment project, reported that one of the latest concepts in treatment of cocaine and other drug abuse in juveniles is the development of recovery high schools. The main focus of these schools is abstinence and recovery for students after a course of inpatient treatment for their addictions. There are thirty recovery high schools around the United States. Andrew Finch, executive director of the Association of Recovery Schools, in an interview with Scheinin, said: "To think a teenager is going to go for treatment for 30 days and then come back to his old environment—where he bought his drugs, where his peers are using, and where he was seen as a drug user . . . that's not realistic for the vast majority of kids. For them, school is the danger zone. It's like an adult alcoholic being required to go to work in a bar." Overall, it seems that recovery schools work. Although 20 to 30 percent of the teens in recovery high schools

These teenagers are enrolling in Hope Academy, a new recovery high school in Indianapolis, Indiana. Abstinence from drug usage is one of the goals of the school.

relapse into drug use, this is far fewer than the number who relapse after other courses of treatment (as many as 80 percent).

Drug abuse cost society $97.7 billion in 1992 and $180.9 billion in 2002. If costs continue to rise at the same rate of 5.3 percent per year, the costs will be almost $320 billion by 2012. And who pays for it? Every man, woman, and child in the United States was taxed $965 to pay the tab in 1992. The cost will be about $1,300 per person in 2012!

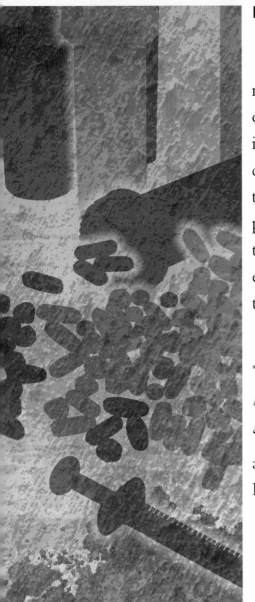

CHAPTER 6
Cocaine and the Media

The media industry includes newspapers, magazines, book publishing, television, cinema, radio, the music industry, and the Internet, among others. The goal of the media is to sell an idea, or goods and services, or a lifestyle. By controlling the information they disseminate, the media have tremendous power to direct people's thinking and can even influence their behavior. The following are a few examples of media influence as it pertains to teens and cocaine.

THE MUSIC INDUSTRY AND COCAINE RAP

"Coke Is It: Rap's Drug Obsession," an article written by Sasha Frere-Jones for the December 25, 2006, issue of the *New Yorker*

Young Jeezy, shown here performing at the 2006 Billboard Music Awards ceremony, frequently raps about possessing and trafficking cocaine.

magazine, is a report on who's who in rap today. It also relates the compulsion of many rappers to boast about using and trafficking cocaine. Frere-Jones wrote, "In September, the magazine *W* announced that cocaine is again a fashionable vice. In pop music, cocaine never went away." He goes on to say that almost every rapper brags of selling cocaine. Hip-hop artists Clipse and Young Jeezy rap almost exclusively about possessing and trafficking cocaine. Cocaine has become so frequent a topic in rap music that a special subcategory of rap has evolved, cocaine rap. A lot of teens listen to cocaine rap. Young Jeezy's first album, for instance, was bought by 1.7 million people in 2005. Are teens listening to rap and enjoying it for what it is—great rhythm, innovative use of music, and vivid poetry? Or, do they take to heart the messages being sent?

FASHION, BEAUTY, AND COCAINE

Thin is beautiful! That is the underlying message of most of the fashion, beauty, and advertising industries. Just look at current issues of *CosmoGIRL!* or *Teen Vogue*. Almost everyone depicted in them is thin. The fashion industry knows that people buy clothes they think will make them look thin because thinness is synonymous with beauty in American culture. Most models who show these clothes are more than thin; they are emaciated. Models maintain their incredibly low weights by not eating or by "purging," and many use cocaine to suppress their appetites to stay thin. In "Cocaine and the Catwalk," an article published in the *Independent* on September 18, 2005, a fashion industry insider was reported to say, "Models use coke like truck drivers do, to stay awake and keep working." Sophie Anderton, a model who used cocaine herself, said in the same article, "Drugs are so accessible within the industry . . . it is very difficult to steer completely clear of them."

In *Northern Life*, a Canadian newspaper, an article entitled "We All Can't Be Angelina" was published in which several girls share their thoughts about the media's obsession with thinness as beauty. One girl said it all: "When teenage girls look at these images, it makes them feel insecure about what they look like. Because all of the famous Hollywood stars look like that, they want to too. All girls want to look like their idols. But when their idols weigh 80 pounds at 5 foot 5, this is not good." It is doubly bad when young women, attempting to emulate their idols, turn to cocaine to help them with weight loss.

MOVIES AND COCAINE

While cocaine use is casually portrayed in many movies, especially those packed with crime and violence, it is also the main subject of many movies. *The Pace That Kills*, released in 1935 and subsequently rereleased as *Cocaine Fiends*, was the first of these movies. It was an antidrug film that focused heavily on moral issues. *Superfly*, *Scarface*, *Clockers*, *Wired*, and *Jumpin' at the Boneyard* are other movies with cocaine use and trafficking as their main topics.

Blow, released in 2001, is based on the life of George Jung, who is credited with starting cocaine trafficking between Colombia and the United States. Instead of emphasizing the incredible disaster cocaine has been to cocaine users and to society as a whole, Jung becomes, inappropriately, a folk hero.

A film released in 2006 called *Cocaine Cowboys* does the same thing—it creates a folk hero of a cocaine trafficker and hitman named Jorge "Rivi" Ayala. According to Jeanette Catsoulis, a movie reviewer for the *New York Times, Cocaine Cowboys* is an "overlong, overexcited, over-the-top . . . account of the blood-drenched Miami drug culture in the 1970s and 1980s." In addition to making a folk hero of Ayala, the film is, in her words, filled with "brutal violence, foul language, and obscene wads of cash."

Cocaine Cowboys, a movie that premiered October 18, 2006, in Miami Beach, Florida, is, according to filmmaker Billy Corben, a history lesson disguised as a gangster film. It recalls the cocaine wars in Miami Beach in the 1970s and 1980s.

The messages these movies bring to young people are mixed. They do show many of the problems of cocaine use, but they also tend to glamorize the "bad guys." Hopefully, the underlying truth of the destructive power of cocaine addiction will become evident when they are viewed critically.

CONCLUSION

Cocaine is an illegal drug and a highly addictive drug. Once hooked, cocaine addicts will do anything to support their habits. Cocaine abusers are at added risk for heart attacks, strokes, severe malnutrition, seizures, paranoia, unplanned pregnancies, hepatitis C, and HIV, not to mention death. Cocaine addiction is extremely hard to kick—there are no alternative medications to help. The possession and trafficking of cocaine are felonies and can lead to a sentence of life imprisonment.

Much information and disinformation continues to be disseminated about cocaine's effect on America's economy and politics. The war on drugs continues to be waged at a huge cost to the American public. Whether it is being won or not, or whether it can ever be won, is an open debate among many segments of society. For now, the best advice you will ever receive about cocaine is expressed in these words from a young cocaine addict: "Don't mess with cocaine, it wins every time."

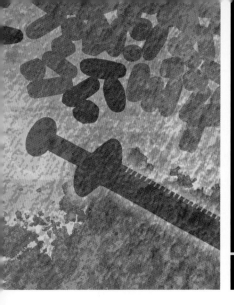

GLOSSARY

cadaver A corpse or dead body.

cartel An association of private business organizations that work together to control the production, sale, and price of a commodity (such as cocaine).

central nervous system The brain and spinal cord.

concoction A mixture made from several different ingredients.

constrict To become narrower or smaller.

cut A slang term meaning to mix a drug with another substance (such as sugar).

denature To modify a substance by heat or chemical means so that it no longer has the properties it previously had.

detoxification Freeing a drug user from an addictive substance in the body or from dependence on or addiction to that substance.

disinformation Knowledge that is not true that is intentionally passed along in order to mislead.

felony A serious crime that frequently results in a fine and/or imprisonment.

freebase Cocaine hydrochloride that has been converted to cocaine sulfate with the use of a solvent to remove additives used in cutting the cocaine.

hunter-gatherers Ancient people who lived by hunting and gathering food, rather than by farming and ranching.

illicit Unlawful; illegal.

line A slang term for a quantity of cocaine to be snorted.

mandatory Required by law; obligatory.

metabolite A substance left behind after a product is broken down in the body.

metric ton A decimal system weight equal to 2,204.6 pounds (1,000 kg).

prestige Power to command admiration; high esteem.

prowess Superiority in ability, skill, or technique.

purging Getting rid of food from the body suddenly and harshly, usually through vomiting, exercise, or laxatives.

pusher A slang term for someone who sells drugs.

solvent A substance, usually a fluid, used to dissolve something.

step on A slang term meaning to cut or mix a drug with another substance (such as sugar).

stimulant A substance that temporarily increases vital activities.

trafficking The manufacture and sale of illegal substances.

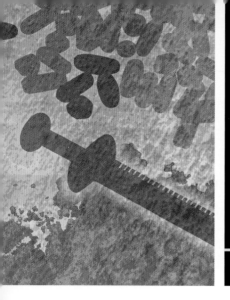

FOR MORE INFORMATION

Canadian Centre on Substance Abuse
75 Albert Street, Suite 300
Ottawa, ON K1P 5E7
Canada
(613) 235-4048
Web site: http://ccsa.ca/CCSA/EN/TopNav/home
This agency provides national leadership and advice to mobilize efforts to reduce alcohol and other drug-related harms.

Center for Substance Abuse Prevention (CSAP)
5600 Fisher's Lane, Room 800
Rockville, MD 20857
(301) 443-0373
Web site: http://www.csap.samhsa.gov
This agency's aim is to promote youth development to reduce risk-taking behaviors across an individual's lifetime.

Center for Substance Abuse Treatment (CSAT)
5600 Fisher's Lane, Room 618

Rockville, MD 20857

(301) 443-0560

Web site: http://www.csat.samhsa.gov

This agency promotes quality and availability of community-based substance abuse treatment services for individuals and families who need them.

National Institute on Drug Abuse (NIDA)

6001 Executive Boulevard, Room 5213

Bethesda, MD 20892-9561

(301) 443-1124

Web site: http://www.nida.nih.gov

NIDA's mission is to lead the nation in bringing the power of science to bear on drug abuse and addiction. It supports research and disseminates information.

WEB SITES

Due to the changing nature of Internet links, Rosen Publishing has developed an online list of Web sites related to the subject of this book. This site is updated regularly. Please use this link to access the list:

http://www.rosenlinks.com/daas/coca

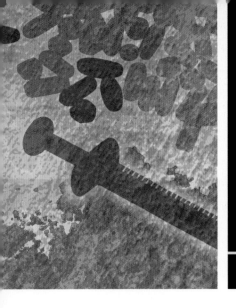

FOR FURTHER READING

Booth, Coe. *Tyrell*. New York, NY: Scholastic Press, 2006.

Ellis, Deborah. *I Am a Taxi*. La Jolla, CA: Groundwork Books, 2006.

Esherick, Joan. *Dying for Acceptance: A Teen's Guide to Drug- and Alcohol-Related Health Issues*. Broomall, PA: Mason Crest Publishing, 2004.

Hyde, Margaret O., and John Setara. *Drugs 101: An Overview for Teens*. Kirkland, WA: 21st Century Publishing, 2003.

Lawton, Sandra, ed. *Drug Information for Teens*. 2nd ed. Detroit, MI: Omnigraphics, 2006.

Moyers, William. *Broken*. New York, NY: Penguin Group, 2006.

Raczek, Linda T. *Teen Addiction*. Farmington Hills, MI: Gale Group, 2003.

Shaw, Brian F., Paul Ritvo, and Jane Irvine. *Addiction and Recovery for Dummies*. Hoboken, NJ: Wiley Publishing, 2005.

Sommers, Michael A. *Cocaine* (Incredibly Disgusting Drugs). New York, NY: Rosen Publishing, 2008.

BIBLIOGRAPHY

Archer, Dennis. "It's Time to Get Smart on Crime." American Bar Association. 2003. Retrieved December 3, 2007 (http://www.abanet.org/media/releases/opedcrime.html).

Arkangel, Carmelito, Jr. "Cocaine Abuse." WebMD. 2007. Retrieved November 20, 2007 (http://www.emedicinehealth.com/Script/main/art.asp?articlekey=58914&pf=3&page=1).

Calderon, Michelle. "Age as Criminal Defense." 2005. Retrieved December 6, 2007 (http://www.anairhoads.org/calderon/agedefense.shtml).

Catsoulis. Jeanette. "Cocaine Cowboys." *New York Times*, October 27, 2006. Retrieved December 24, 2007 (http://www.movies.nytimes.com/2006/10/27/movies/27cowb.html?fta=y).

EurekAlert. "$2.2M INH Grant to Develop Drugs to Suppress Cocaine Cravings." November 16, 2007. Retrieved November 17, 2007 (http://www.eurekalert.org/pub_rcleases/2007-11/uoia-mn111607.php).

Federal Bureau of Investigation. *Crime in the United States, 2006.* 2007. Retrieved December 14, 2007 (http://www.fbi.gov/ucr/cius2006/data/table_36.html).

Frere-Jones, Sasha. "Coke Is It: Rap's Drug Obsession." *New Yorker*, Vol. 82, No. 43, December 25, 2006, pp. 146–147.

Hoover's, Inc. "Overview." Hoover's Reports on Coca-Cola, the Gap, McDonald's, and Nike. 2007. Retrieved December 21, 2007 (http://www.hoovers.com).

Independent. "Cocaine and the Catwalk." September 18, 2005. Retrieved November 29, 2007 (http://www.cocaine.org/misc/catwalk.html).

Karp, Sarah. "State Drug Law Hits City Teens, Minorities." *Chicago Reporter*, May 2000.

King's College, London, England. "Genetic Cause for Cocaine Addiction." March 13, 2007. Retrieved December 2, 2007 (http://www.kcl.ac.uk/phpnews/wmview.php?ArtID=1166).

Marks, Alexandra. "Revised Guidelines Lessen Disparity in Prison Terms for Crack Versus Powder." *Christian Science Monitor*, November 2, 2007. Retrieved December 2, 2007 (http://www.csmonitor.com/2007/1102/p01s02-usju.htm).

Myers, Anessa. "Emergency Room Visits Helping Drive Up Health Care Expenses." *Goldsboro News Argus*, July 31, 2007. Retrieved December 8, 2007 (http://www.newsargus.com/news/archives/2007/07/31/emergency_room_visits_helping_drive_up_health_care_expenditures/index.shtml).

National Drug Intelligence Center. *National Drug Threat Assessment 2006.* January 2006. Retrieved March 14, 2008 (http://www.usdoj.gov/ndic/pubs11/18862/index.htm).

National Institute of Justice. *Drug Courts: The Second Decade.* June 2006. Retrieved December 3, 2007 (http://www.ojp. usdoj.gov/nij/pubs-sum/211081.htm).

National Institute of Mental Health. "Teenage Brain: A Work in Progress." 2001. Retrieved January 30, 2008 (http:// www.nimh.nih.gov/health/publications/teen-brain-a-work-in-progress.shtml).

National Institute on Drug Abuse. "NIDA InfoFacts: Crack and Cocaine." 2006. Retrieved November 15, 2007 (http://www. nida.nih.gov/Infofacts/cocaine.html).

National Institute on Drug Abuse. "NIDA InfoFacts: Drugged Driving." 2007. Retrieved November 17, 2007 (http://www. nida.nih.gov/Infofacts/driving.html).

News-Medical.net. "D-cycloserine Could Help Treat Drug Addiction." November 7, 2007. Retrieved December 1, 2007 (http://www.news-medical.net/?id=32293).

Northern Life. "We All Can't Be Angelina." November 16, 2007. Retrieved December 16, 2007 (http://www.northernlife.ca/ News/Opinions/2007/11-16-07-teens.html).

Office of National Drug Control Policy. "The Economic Costs of Drug Abuse in the United States 1992–2002." 2004. Retrieved December 10, 2007 (http://www.whitehousedrugpolicy.gov/ publications/economic_costs/economic_costs/pdf).

Office of National Drug Control Policy. "Juveniles and Drugs." 2006. Retrieved December 6, 2007 (http://www. whitehousedrugpolicy.gov/drugfact/juvenile/index.html).

Ritter, Malcomb. "Study: Immaturity May Spark Teen Crime." Associated Press, December 1, 2007. Retrieved December 3, 2007 (http://ap.google.com/article/ALeqM5jr4zphAlmolpl WJ7BZE2UiflolzQD8T9ELRGO).

Robert Woods Johnson Foundation. "Illicit Drug Policies: Selected Laws from 50 States." 2002. Retrieved November 30, 2007 (http://www.rwjf.org/pr/product.jsp?ia=131&id=14208).

Scheinin, Richard. "1.6 Million Addicted Kids Shaping Outside the Box Treatment Strategies." Robert Woods Johnson Foundation. Retrieved December 8, 2007 (http://stories. silenttreatment.info/youth_01.asp).

Substance Abuse and Mental Health Services Administration. "Drug Data Summary." March 2003. Retrieved December 17, 2007 (http://www.whitehousedrugpolicy.gov/publications/ factsht/drugdate/index/html).

Substance Abuse and Mental Health Services Administration. "Results of the 2006 National Survey on Drugs and Health." 2006. Retrieved December 23, 2007 (http://www.oas.samhsa. gov/nsduh/2k6nsduh/2k6results.cfm).

United Nations Office on Drugs and Crime. *World Drug Report 2007*. June 2007. Retrieved January 8, 2008 (http://www. unodc/en/data–and–analysis/WDR_2007.html).

INDEX

ABOUT THE AUTHOR

Linda Bickerstaff, MD, a University of Missouri–trained general surgeon and a Mayo-trained peripheral vascular surgeon, has vivid memories and a few nightmares about teens she cared for in emergency and operating rooms following their drugged driving sprees. She also remembers with admiration those, who with a lot of effort, kicked their habits and started the lifelong road to recovery.

PHOTO CREDITS

Pp. 5, 33 DEA; p. 8 Aizar Raldes/AFP/Getty Images; p. 10 Library of Congress Prints and Photographs Division; p. 13 Jodi Cobb/National Geographic/Getty Images; p. 16 Antonio Scorza/AFP/Getty Images; p. 17 Alfredo Estrella/AFP/Getty Images; p. 21 © www.istockphoto.com/ johanna goodyear; p. 25 © Brookhaven National Laboratory/Photo Researchers, Inc.; p. 28 © John Birdsall/The Image Works; p. 30 © Larry Mulvehill/The Image Works; pp. 34, 40, 47 © AP Images; p. 37 © Larry Kolvoord/The Image Works; p. 43 © Bob Daemmrich/The Image Works; p. 49 Kevin Winter/Fox/Getty Images; p. 52 Gustavo Caballero/ Getty Images.

Designer: Tahara Anderson; Editor: Kathy Kuhtz Campbell
Photo Researcher: Amy Feinberg